D1104579

Special Methods for Attaining Spiritual Mastery

BY GEORGE LeROY DALE

UNITY SCHOOL OF CHRISTIANITY
LEE'S SUMMIT, MO.
1958

Special Methods for
Attaining Spiritual Mastery
was first published in 1956.
This is the second printing.

This is one of a series of Unity books devoted to teaching how you can make your life better by applying Christian principles. The first Unity book, *Lessons in Truth,* was published in 1894 and is still in publication. The Unity work itself was established in 1889, when its founders, Charles and Myrtle Fillmore, began to share with others the Truth that had helped them.

The Unity movement now reaches millions of persons all over the world. Unity School of Christianity includes the Silent Unity department, to which thousands of people each year write for prayers for any need, and the Publishing Department, which distributes the Unity books and magazines that carry the Unity message around the world. Unity centers and churches are located in many large cities.

FOREWORD

"Exercise Class at 11:30 a.m."

For those who have attended Unity Training School, the words will recall many happy and profitable hours spent in the classes conducted by Dr. George LeRoy Dale.

Dr. Dale has made a unique contribution to the Unity work through his position as Registrar of the Training School. Students throughout the years have found his attitude always helpful and encouraging. In former years he was a physical-culture director, and he found many ways to put this experience to good use in exercise classes. He has a truly wonderful way of combining metaphysical teaching with his exercises, thus illustrating and emphasizing the important principles presented. There is never any strained effort. Everything moves along easily, rhythmically, and joyously, and all who take part feel refreshed and renewed. In short, the exercise classes are times of inspiration and uplift, with a corresponding enrichment of consciousness.

The exercises and songs contained in this book are those actually used in Dr.

Dale's classes, and when systematically practiced will bring about beneficial results.

Dr. Dale in his daily life and activities exemplifies the physical and metaphysical aspects of his teaching. He thoroughly believes in and practices the Golden Rule in all its aspects. A student once remarked, "Any man who needs a friend, and looks to Dr. Dale, never looks in vain!" Certainly George LeRoy Dale's friendly spirit permeates this helpful little book; and those who put into practice what is herein suggested will find that these are indeed *Special Methods for Attaining Spiritual Mastery.*

HERBERT J. HUNT

(We gratefully give credit to the various Unity leaders, students, and workers who wrote the words to some of the songs contained herein.)

CONTENTS

SPECIAL METHODS FOR ATTAINING SPIRITUAL MASTERY

What God Is

IN THE dictionaries, in religious books, in pulpits, in schools and colleges, men have given their personal opinions concerning the nature of God.

From the time of the cave man to this modern day, human conceptions of God have varied from "disturbances of nature" to "the quietness beyond human comprehension." Metaphysicians define God as Supreme Being; universal Creator of heaven, earth, and other planets; Creator of all forms of life everywhere; Spirit; unchangeable Principle; unchangeable Law; infinite Peace; divine Love; unadulterated Truth; Divine Mind; unlimited ideas of goodness; perfect invisible action; science of music and numbers; Producer of growth and expansion; unlimited Substance; Heavenly Father; the Source of all goodness and purity; divine all-knowing Intelli-

gence; all-protecting Presence; Omnis-
cience; Omnipresence; Omnipotence;
the all-compassionate One; the universal Thinker and Planner; and so on.

Some persons may still think of God
as having a good and bad nature, and
hope to please Him by certain actions;
but those who have studied Truth have
gone far beyond such a concept. Truth
students know that the one supreme
Power is everywhere and that all
forms of life live and move and have
their being in It.

Mankind probably refers to God as
"He" because in ages past men did
most of the thinking and regarded
women largely as chattels. In the present age however women have come into their own privileges of thinking and
a balanced way of living is coming
forth on the earth. God is just as much
"She" as "He" (as much Mother as
Father), and can be most aptly described as containing all forms of life

regardless of whether male or female forms are manifesting through the vegetable, animal, or human kingdoms.

A person who becomes illumined through the study of Truth is fortunate. His concept of God has grown to a consciousness of understanding that God is everywhere and also within himself; that he is within God; that his own personal thought can enter into and receive a response from God (described by Jesus Christ as our heavenly Father); and that God who has individualized Himself in man can control and direct man's life when man turns to Him.

What Man Is

GOD-MIND, containing all goodness, created man out of Its own life substance by Its own perfect action, and endowed man with unlimited thinking ability. This Son-of-God man has a perfect spiritual body. The spiritual body of this perfect Son-of-God man contains unlimited power. This body is the temple of God for man, "not made with hands."

This spiritual body whose home is in "heaven" (in the highest realm of living), by taking advantage of human conception methods reproduces for itself a physical covering or body of flesh (very much the same as animal bodies in function and structure.)

Jesus said, "Is it not written in your law, I said, Ye are gods?" His teaching that all men created by God have equal privileges of soul development was not favorably received by selfish-minded, influential persons of His time, hence their efforts to destroy both Him and His teaching by causing the death of His physical body through crucifixion. But this only resulted in the further expansion of His teaching that "the kingdom of God is within you," which is the basis of Unity and many other teachings of this age.

As God individualized His nature in all spiritual beings, He created and gave thinking ability to all. All people have at their command God ideas of life, love, truth, energy, power, joy, peace, order, substance, and protection, to help them to have an enjoyable life.

As the mental side of man, functioning through the brain of the physical body, becomes illumined, man finds he really has dominion over the animal and vegetable world, but *not* over his fellow man. Many leaders have assumed power over their fellow men and produced all kinds of discord, wars, diseases, and troubles on earth. The mass of mankind, ignorant of Truth, usually follow leaders as sheep follow shepherds.

A thinker who has prayed faithfully for illumination and opened the way from his own mental realm into his soul nature, where God is always present, does not follow blindly the self-appointed or elected leaders of the race, but obeys divine laws as God reveals them to him. Thus man progresses, always in harmonious agreement with God and his fellow men who are also on the pathway of unfoldment.

The following statements are for personal spiritual unfoldment:

———

As I yield my intellect to Spirit, divine intelligence illumines my mind, guides me in all studies, and shows me clearly what to think, say, and do every day.

———

Divine love harmonizes me with the good in people, things, and conditions all the time.

———

God-substance abundantly supplies all my physical and financial needs day after day.

What Spiritual Learning Is

THE ordinary method of education is to introduce into the mind from without that which is considered proper, right, and beneficial from the human viewpoint.

Kindergartens, grammar schools, high schools, colleges, and universities all offer courses of instruction, arranged by humans who have used reason, attention, will, desire, and judgment of the conscious mind in relation to giving instructions to young and old.

Jesus Christ, the greatest of all mystics, prophets, or spiritual teachers, no doubt at times found it quite difficult to make people understand that what He called the "kingdom of God" was within and around man, and that this kingdom was always ready to respond to man's righteous thought or use of it.

At the time of Jesus' physical life on earth, the human race was at a low

ebb; wars between nations and ignorance of proper living habits were
rampant. His instructions about correct
thinking and living were not generally
understood by the masses of people,
but degree by degree, more and more
of the Truth He taught has come into
use. In this day and age many people
are convinced that it is possible to
study and apply His teachings in such
a way as to have a life of health, happiness, prosperity, and protection.

Spiritual learning is the taking of
ideas, principles, and laws of God into
the mentality of man until man's
whole scheme of living (mentally and
physically) is changed.

This "taking on" (sometimes called
a "conversion," a "change of consciousness," an "illumination," a "saving the soul," a "putting on the new
man,") relates to a higher Power than
the human coming into expression
through the mind and brain of man.

A study of the teachings of Jesus
Christ reveals that it is possible for
man to "tune in" his mind to the one
creative Mind of God and receive
direct inspiration from above. This
process can be called spiritual learning, as it has to do with higher radi-
ations of an eternal, always right-
acting spiritual power which created
man and maintains him spiritually and
perfectly in all conditions of life, here
and hereafter.

Therefore in order to learn spiritually let us repeat often to ourselves
the following statements:

———

I am a perfect spiritual being,
created by God.

———

God has given me a perfect thinking nature, with freedom of
thought.

I have spiritual perception; I have spiritual intuition; I have spiritual understanding.

As the offspring of God, I am one with divine intelligence, one with divine love, one with divine order, one with divine peace, one with divine substance, one with divine motion, one with divine sound, one with divine harmony, one with divine life, one with divine energy, one with divine joy, one with divine power, one with divine will, one with divine freedom, one with divine justice, one with Truth.

I am eternal, limitless, deathless, spaceless, timeless, tireless.

I understand clearly the teachings of Jesus Christ and all other great souls.

I am sensitive, obedient, receptive to Divine Mind ideas only.

———

I have perfect spiritual control over my thoughts, feelings, actions, and reactions.

———

Through divine intelligence, I know all I need to know when I need to know it.

———

I have a perfect memory as a gift from God.

———

I have a perfect conscious phase of mind in which reason, attention, will, desire, and judgment function perfectly.

———

I have a perfect subconscious phase of mind which assures that my appetite, digestion, circulation, assimilation, nutrition, elimination, muscle, joint, bone, nerve, and glandular action function perfectly through my physical body, keeping it in perfect health.

———

As a spiritual being, I have perfect control over my conscious mind, my subconscious mind, my physcial body, and my affairs.

———

I have a perfect imaginative power of mind and I picture only what is good.

———

I have a perfect memory for people, things, and conditions.

How to Become Spiritually Educated

THE word *educate* comes from the Latin word *educare* which means "to bring forth," and relates to attaining knowledge. Knowledge as acquired through ordinary schooling is something pressed into the mind from without, accepted, and memorized. One who has accumulated a great deal of knowledge is often called an "intellectual."

Ordinary education is the transference of instruction from one mind to another. Spiritual education is the fusing of man's mentality and his God-created Spirit, which knows all and has all power to release ideas of life, love, truth, substance, protection, energy, and vitality upon the mental request of man.

Jesus' teachings are clear in regard to demonstration: "Ask, and it shall be given you; seek, and ye shall find; knock, and it shall be opened unto you." The asking, seeking, knocking is the action of mental man (often called the conscious mind) to make his request known to his higher self, the God within, which being the offspring of universal or God-Mind (the Father) can respond or send the power (ideas), so demonstration will take place.

Let us always remember: There is only one power, but we use it in multitudinous ways. The one power of God that we think with, we also use in breathing, seeing, hearing, smelling, touching, tasting, digesting food, rebuilding body cells, eliminating impurities, moving our bodies around. The one power is everywhere, always awaiting our use of it in *all* ways.

This great truth, when discovered by Truth seekers, clears up much mental confusion. Personal responsibility for what each individual thinks, says, and does must be assumed by the individual. "Ignorance of the law is no excuse."

H. Emilie Cady, in her book *Lessons in Truth,* reveals the method of prayer she used in letting the Spirit educate her mentally. Anyone who is willing to pray can achieve like results. It is not difficult; it is easy.

Use the following statements:

———

Thine almighty intelligence in me, Spirit, is revealing to me what to think, say, and do every day, thereby spiritualizing my intellect.

———

The all-knowing, all-understanding, all-informing Mind of God reveals to me why, how, and when I should act in every situation.

Thy divine love is harmonizing me with the good in things, people, and conditions every day. Thine ever-present substance is abundantly supplying all my financial and physical needs every day.

Thy life, joy, harmony, peace, and health find full and perfect expression through me every day.

Thou doth reveal the divine design of my life to me and I manifest it part by part every day.

How to Declare the Truth to Oneself

" AS he [man] thinketh within himself, so is he" is a statement often quoted by Truth teachers and students. It is often explained as a condition that occurs when one thinks and feels subconsciously and manifests what he has thought.

Another metaphysical statement is "As man declares the Truth about God and himself, so does he become."

God is. Spiritual man, His offspring, is. Spiritual man can think and discover the God power in himself, and as he declares it working through him, so does he become or manifest that which he has thought. Each of us is a spiritual being. Jesus said, "Ye shall know the truth, and the truth shall make you free."

The study of Truth is the most important of all studies because through

28

it a life of intelligence, love, peace, joy, safety, and plenty can be enjoyed. The hordes of erroneous thoughts that man holds in his mind can be dissipated by his own words. To some this is almost unbelievable. One may ask, "Is it possible that I of myself can dissipate from my nature all that should not be?" Yes, indeed, it is true! Anyone who can think intelligently can invoke the God of himself (the Christ, the activity of Truth), through his own consciousness, through his own conscious and subconscious phase of mind, through his own brain and nervous system, into and through his own physical body and affairs. He need only try it in order to prove it. These statements can be meditated on for that purpose:

I am the spiritual master of my mind, my body, my affairs.

As a spiritual master I consciously invoke God's laws to bring into operation whatever is good for me.

I no longer just think about things, I declare the Truth of my own spiritual nature and thereby free myself from all that should not be for me.

Health, wealth, happiness in my home, work, and human relationships are all pictures in my consciousness which can be changed for the better as I declare the truth about my higher (Christ) self.

The Truth of God and man reveals itself to me as I seek it. I rejoice in God's guidance through my mind, showing me what to think, what to read, how to live healthfully, how to demonstrate plenty in service and finances.

———

People, things, and conditions have no power to disturb me. I am always poised and centered in the one infinite mind of peace and harmony.

How to Meditate and Go into the Silence

MEDITATION, *silence, treatment,* and *prayer work* are all terms that are used by various Truth teachers and students to describe methods of contact with infinite Mind.

There is, however, a difference in the various methods of approach to and contact with God. Meditation is the act of using the conscious mind to become aware of the meaning of a Truth statement. When a student meditates, he considers what a statement means. For example, if the statement is, *I am a child of God and God life is flowing through me constantly,* the student could review in his mind what the terms "I am a child of God" and "God life" mean to him, and he would thereby be meditating on or gaining the meaning of the statement. The meaning would then be a mental picture, which would become a part of his subconscious mind. By impressing his subconscious mind, the student sets certain laws of expression into action, and a manifestation or outworking takes place through and around him.

Slowly or rapidly repeating a statement can be called treatment or prayer work. Impressing the subconscious mind with a repeated statement or prayer (after meditation) results in subconscious action taking place. It may be likened to the washing of an exposed photographic film in a dark container of chemical solution. When the film is outlined and printed, a clear picture appears. This is what transpires in one's subconscious mind when he tries to produce through his own body or affairs a picture or experience that he desires.

Thought controls emotion or feeling. Thought can be used to reduce, change, dissolve, or intensify a feeling.

If it were not for this gift of God to us, we would never be able to describe an inner feeling by voice or written word. To think with feeling and truly impress the subconsciousness, quickly and deeply, results in quick manifestation or results.

Of course, one who desires to demonstrate should always study Truth (particularly the teachings of Jesus) in order to know consciously how to word his righteous desires, so that the results will be beneficial to himself and others.

The silence is a condition in which conscious thinking and body action or motion are stilled as much as possible to *let God take over*. This can be practiced at any time, anywhere, either before or after a definite prayer or treatment period.

God-Mind operates in quietness and stillness and reveals its ideas to its offspring (man) on request. We pray to

God; God responds to us in the silence; and then up through the subconscious and conscious phases of mind comes the response. At times, through the operation of divine law, conditions develop or appear *around* us to prove that God has heard and all is well.

Responsibility for the use of thought and feeling is personal to everyone on earth. Hence the necessity of understanding what is meant when one says, "I only want for myself what I am willing that all people may have at the same time, and I pray that God will guide me in all my thinking."

How to Achieve Happiness in Human Relationships

TO some people happiness means enjoyment of physical sense life, plenty of money to spend, and having one's own way in all of life's activities. Some who find they cannot have their own way at all times often complain bitterly, accusing others of interfering with their desires or rights.

Humanity on the whole is slowly emerging from the competitive, selfish mode of life that is represented by the racial mind vibrations which have found subconscious outlets through most people.

A marriage usually takes place because a man and woman in love believe that happiness will develop through living together under one roof, having children, raising a family, and entering into all the various activities that have to do with churches,

36

schools, work, entertainment, travel, and so forth. But some persons are still seeking happiness, even after many years of married life.

Those who are illumined by Truth study have discovered how to bring the conscious and subconscious activities of their own natures under the control of Spirit, and have found that real happiness consists in letting the "joy of the Lord" have its way through man. In other words divine joy (as part of Divine Mind) will respond to man's prayers for happiness and will radiate through man all day long.

Simple, practical prayer statements can be used to induce happiness. Say often:

———

I let go all selfish desires concerning myself or others.

———

I refuse to let feelings of unhappiness dominate my life. I cast out all unhappy vibrations.

I grant forgiveness and freedom to all people to enjoy life just as I wish to enjoy my own.

Knowing my happiness comes not from others but from God, I let the joy of the Lord have full play through me every day.

The joy of the Lord radiates through the mental and physical atmosphere of my home and business every day.

How to Understand and Practice the Golden Rule

ADVICE as to practicing the Golden Rule has been presented to the race mind for ages, long before the physical birth of Jesus on earth. Ancient Hindu and Chinese philosophers and teachers were emphatic in teaching that the Golden Rule is the basis of proper human relationships. In our present age we read much about why the Golden Rule should be practiced by national leaders, politicians, religious sects, and industrial organizations.

In fact, almost all of us admire the Golden Rule philosophy and think it a wonderful thing for the other fellow to follow! But surface thinking brings little return in changing character and subconscious actions and reactions. It is the training of the personal subconscious mind by each individual that re-

sults in the automatic Golden Rule reaction taking place in situations con-
fronting the individual.

"All things . . . whatsoever ye would
that men should do unto you, even so
do ye also unto them: for this is the
law and the prophets." Doing to others
as you would have others do to you re-
quires a thinking through clearly and a
control of emotions, a personally accepted responsibility for your own
thought and reaction. Can you remain
calm if someone calls you a liar or
cheat when it is an unjust accusation?
Can you look on the troubles of the
world and see that each person's
troubles start in his own mind, and
that redemption and deliverance can
come only through personally con-
trolled subconscious change? Can you
cease blaming ancestors, national leaders, or even God Himself for the circumstances around you? If you can,
you are to be congratulated, because

the indications are that you have discovered a great truth: namely, to do
first to others in personal thought and
action that which you wish done to
you.

In other words, you have found that
thinking produces mental images that
invoke laws bringing back to each one
the results or manifestations of his
thoughts (or what he has accepted
from others.)

Approximately five hundred years
before Christ, Confucius, the great phi-
losopher and teacher of ancient China,
advocated the Golden Rule as the Rule
of Wisdom for personal unfoldment
and also the rule to be taught to all
emperors, judges, and others in authority in the Chinese Empire. Confucius is
credited with having so educated the
rulers of a certain province through
Golden Rule practice that jails were
emptied in two years and judges and
lawyers had no work to do! Crime and

war had disappeared because of the right mental training given to all people of that province.

What happened in those days can happen again in our modern age if enough people learn to love and practice the Golden Rule. Think what would happen if enough people who understand correct principles of thinking and acting would pray definitely for the illumination of all governmental officials over the earth!

What we send out comes back to us. As we learn to practice the Golden Rule until it becomes a subconscious habit, it attracts back to us what we send out. To do this successfully a series of prayer statements will help wonderfully:

———

I do first just what I would have others do to me. I do not do for others what they are unwilling to do for themselves. I refuse to accept (consciously or subconsciously) any person's opinion of me not based on Truth. I no longer hold anyone in bondage with my personal thoughts or feelings or actions. I express and ask for forgiveness whenever necessary. I love God with all my mind and heart, and I love my neighbor as I love my higher self.

———

Every day, I pray that all leaders of all nations and all people in positions of human authority become illumined and practice the Golden Rule in all their activities.

How to Enjoy Peace on Earth

THE yearning for peace by most of the two billion or more people on earth will sooner or later bring peace on earth. Political efforts, national treaties, trade exchanges, sermons by ministers of all faiths, discussions by radio and television performers, debates by educators and students—all tend in the direction of peace on earth.

But how few realize that the subconscious race habit of the ages of killing animals and people in wars is part of the subconscious race mind which encircles the earth invisibly and which controls masses of people who are ignorant of personal responsibility for their thinking and acting. It has been said that what is inside must come out, and we know that the pressure of subconscious error wells up through the race mind causing wars and diseases of all kinds. Destructive, fearful, lack-of-love thinking brings terrible retribution through mankind.

This can all be corrected by scientific prayer work by those who desire betterment of conditions. Jesus Christ realized Himself as a Son of God and taught that the kingdom of God (peace, love, intelligence, right action) is within man. So each person can do likewise: seek the Father within, allow Divine Mind to have its way and thereby be assured of a peaceful, loving life. The peace of God as a radiance through and around each person will come forth as a response to individual prayer work. When a few people realize this and pray individually and collectively, the impression made on Divine Mind brings its response.

What one or a few can do, all can do, since God is impartial and unchangeable Mind and is the Father of peace, love, intelligence, and supply

for all. The Golden Rule of right personal action for everyone applies to
man's relationship to animals as well
as to his fellow men. Hence the following prayer statements, if faithfully
used, will so change the consciousness
that peace on earth, good will to all
men, can become possible:

**I join my personal thought with
the thoughts of all peace-minded
people in all nations over the earth
and affirm that God-peace, God-
love, God's one perfect action is
manifesting through all people who
are willing to let it do so.**

**The killing of men and animals is
no longer part of my consciousness.**

The freedom I desire for myself is

the freedom I grant to all God-created creatures on earth.

———

God-peace, released by my personal thought within myself, assures peace of mind and action for me, and adds to the peace in the world.

———

The peace which "passeth all understanding" is deep within me and comes forth through all my personal activities.

How to Stay Young, Strong, and Healthy

DISEASE beliefs, feelings, impressions, and conditions of the race mind may seep into the subconscious nature of some persons more insidiously after the age of forty. Such error thoughts reap their toll.

Fortunate is the Truth student who understands this and who knows how to prevent it by definitely training his own subconsciousness to refuse to accept such errors.

The majority of Truth students have passed the forty-year mark before they become sufficiently interested to rise above racial emotions and take charge of their own thinking and body habits.

The necessity of making changes in living habits causes many people to take up the study of Truth. The racial-mind tendency to blame parents, doctors, ministers, or politicians for one's troubles disappears when Truth is discovered within and opportunities to demonstrate are revealed.

The constant reproduction of cells in our physical bodies goes on year after year. If the mental images of youth, strength, and health are planted subconsciously day after day, undoubtedly longevity will result. The subconscious mind is the master of the physical body, and that same subconsciousness is the servant of the conscious mind; and both the conscious and the subconscious mind are servants of God in man. Thought connects all phases of man's nature. Jesus said: "Verily I say unto you, Except ye turn, and become as little children, ye shall in no wise enter into the kingdom of heaven. Whosoever therefore shall humble himself as this little child, the same is the greatest in the kingdom of heaven."

If adults could free themselves in-

stantly of false beliefs involving responsibilities concerning their lives
and affairs, they would find themselves
young and strong again. However, it is
necessary to study Truth to find out
how to do this, and then to let the
Truth work in mind so that changes
will take place in body chemistry and
action, and divine life flow freely
again through man.

Willingness to seek the kingdom
of God within is absolutely necessary
in the effort to rediscover and enjoy
youth, health, and strength year after
year.

Some people have discovered that
special diets, special exercises, sufficient rest, and a right mental attitude
are very helpful in regaining health.
The various actions and reactions to
such treatment show the effect of mind
on or through the body, because when
the mind (or soul) withdraws or sepa-
rates entirely from the body, the body

is dead. Hence the statement, "The mental (or soul) reaction to the treatment determines the effect in the body," is absolutely correct.

A short cut to releasing youth, health, and strength through the body can be made by treatment or scientific prayer work, either by a practitioner or oneself. To sit down and quietly train one's subconsciousness with one's personal thought, using Truth statements, will bring, sooner or later, marvelous changes in body habits, body chemistry, function, and structure.

In Unity classes instruction is often given in control of the body by the "word." The following are some of the statements used.

(Concentrate attention in different parts of the body as the "word" is spoken three times.)

I am youthful, strong, well, har-

monious through my (front brain)
(eyes) (ears) (nose) (mouth)
(throat) (back brain and spinal
column) (heart) (lungs) (solar
plexus) (stomach) (intestines)
(colon) (rectum) (liver) (gall
bladder) (pancreas) (spleen) (kidneys) (bladder) (generative or-
gans) (hips) (thighs) (knees)
(lower legs) (feet) (all arteries,
veins, capillaries) (bones and
joints) (glands and membranes)
(nerves) (muscles) (skin) (hair)
(nails).

I am youthful, well, and harmonious through and through and
through.

Youth, health, strength are God's
gifts to me and I manifest them
every day.

Old age, diseases are only mate-
rialized erroneous beliefs. I now dissipate them by my words of Truth,
and youth, health, strength, longevity are mine.

How to Eat for Health

IN modern-day advertising one can find unlimited varieties of opinions and ideas concerning diet, offered by food manufacturing companies, doctors, health lecturers, health writers and advisers. All of these persons are quite sincere, no doubt, in their work of trying to help men "eat their way to health."

The God-power that created us gave us ability to think, intelligence to use, eyes to see with, and appetite when hunger is to be appeased. That same Power placed on earth plenty of wonderful food in the form of grains, fruits, vegetables, nuts, berries, and animal products of various kinds, from which it is possible for man to select what appeals to him as suitable nourishment for his physical body.

The author has had the experience of counseling with health-seekers of all ages, and can truthfully say that he knows of no one particular article of food, no one particular dietary method that can accomplish for all the restoration of health. Different people are in different states of consciousness (awareness of thought and feeling). Consciousness should govern eating habits.

Physical ancestral tendencies through heredity, eating habits acquired through environmental surroundings, emotional subconscious reactions of the individual, educational opportunities, all have to be considered in counseling people concerning eating for health. Those whose parents have been meat-eaters all their physical lives and are not yet ready to give up meat eating usually suffer and feel worse when placed on a non-meat diet because their subconscious nature has not been changed. But when people become spiritually educated through Truth study, a change of consciousness takes place. It becomes easy then to bring appetite and eating habits under the control of the Spirit of God within by using simple prayers such as:

———

The intelligence of God guides me through my mind, through my appetite, through my sense of smell and sight, and I eat only the foods that are best for my bodily health. As I grow into more spiritual understanding, I easily let go all thoughts and desires that have to do with all kinds of killing (including the killing of animals for food and clothing) and I rejoice in Golden Rule living.

———

I eat not too much, not too little, but just sufficient of God-created foods for my bodily needs.

My subconscious knows my bodily needs and it operates perfectly through my mind, eyes, sense of taste and smell, and I never overeat.

———

My bowels, lungs, kidneys, skin function perfectly, eliminating all waste, and I express God-health constantly.

———

I am not disturbed by anyone's personal opinion concerning my eating.

———

I am never worried over others' opinions about my health. I am at peace always.

———

All desires for more food than necessary are dissolved out of my mind, and obese appearances disappear.

Divine intelligence reveals to me all I need to know about fasting, dieting, and food combinations.

———

Divine intelligence slenderizes [or stoutens] my physical body safely, quickly, easily, and gracefully.

———

The divine image of a beautiful physical body of perfect proportions and perfect functioning, implanted in my soul in the beginning by God, now comes into manifestation.

How to Breathe for Health

"GOD is the breath of my life" is a statement that is a fact in relation to living on earth. God *is* the breath of life to all His creations— vegetable, animal, human. When any organized form of life stops breathing, death comes to that form and a withering process follows until finally the law of "dust unto dust" is fulfilled.

Charles Fillmore said that all things that mankind needs are "in the air" ready to manifest or be used on demand. Our atmosphere contains hydrogen, oxygen, nitrogen, and other life sustaining elements, which can be drawn in greater degree into our physical bodies through special breathing exercises. Artificial respiration in cases of drowning, the "iron lung" action in cases of polio victims, the taking in of big gulps of breath by athletes before making strenuous efforts, all indicate that the life force or energy in the air can be contacted and used for revitalizing and energizing the body.

During sleep most people breathe much more deeply than when awake, and this subconscious deep breathing action has much to do with the storing up of energy or vitality in the brain, glands, and nerve centers of the body for use the following day. Shallow breathers do not usually manifest good health or energetic action. Anyone who desires to do so can learn to use a few simple breathing exercises, combined with affirmations, that will result in quick chemical changes (metabolism) taking place in the physical body.

In the classes taught in the Unity Training School, the author has trained many students, combining mental action and physical breathing under spiritual direction so that the whole man—spirit, soul, and body—expresses as a complete unit of vigorous life and power. There need be no fear about becoming "too psychic" through these breathing exercises. A positive mind directed toward expressing God-life vigorously and righteously cannot be influenced detrimentally.

The student can assume a standing, sitting, or reclining position. If indoors, the room should be well ventilated. Inhalation should take place through the nose, exhalation through either the nose or the mouth.

Exercise I

Close one nostril; breathe in and out ten or more times. Affirm silently or audibly:

The inflow and outflow of God-life and substance through me is unrestricted and free.

Repeat, using the other nostril. Then

alternate left and right nostril breathing.

Exercise II

Breathe in deeply through both
nostrils, hold breath, vibrate the diaphragm vigorously. The silent affirmation to use is:

God-life force is flowing through
every part of my body, revitalizing
and rebuilding every part perfectly.

Relax and quietly exhale.

How to Sleep for Body Revitalization

ALL organized forms of life need periods of sleep. Man usually needs six to eight hours sleep out of each twenty-four. If he does not get enough sleep, disease and weakness often result.

In our youthful days, before responsibilities become a large issue in our lives, sleep comes naturally. But as our minds develop and the battle of destructive thinking versus constructive thinking affects our subconscious nature, sleep or thorough relaxation is interfered with, and many of us find ourselves seeking the help of physicians.

God gives all His creatures peaceful sleep. But man has so abused his gifts from God that he usually has to undergo suffering before he finds the way back to his Father within (the kingdom of God).

Insomnia can be caused by erroneous thinking habits; financial worries about the past, present, or future; irritations; frustrations; abuses of the sexual nature; guilty conscience; overeating and improper foods; lack of proper exercise and deep breathing resulting in bodily toxemia; fears about death or disease. All of these false beliefs and many others make up the race-mind vibrations that seep into the subconscious nature of man night and day, robbing him of the rest that God intended for him.

Therefore it is wise to train the subconscious mind with affirmations that will cause the human body to be vitalized by thought and breath during sleep.

The following can be repeated gently before sleeping:

I relax in mind and body in order to sleep.

———

I let go of every erroneous thought and feeling of the day's experience.

———

I radiate love to all people, forgive all mistakes, and I shall sleep peacefully all night.

———

During sleep, God's protection is mine; nothing shall disturb me. Deep breathing will take place.

———

While I sleep, God will revitalize every part of my being. I will awaken refreshed and renewed, ready for another day's activity in God's physical workshop.

How to Improve Eyesight

TRULY it has been said that the eyes are "the windows of the soul." They are also the physical cameras of the body. We, as spiritual beings, through our physical eyes look out into the natural world, take pictures, and interpret them, all in a flash (so to speak).

In reality, there is only one Presence, one Power, one perfect, right action of God taking place throughout the universe, although to our physical senses it seems as if there are both good and evil powers, and often we seem to be trying to find out which is which. In God we "live, and move, and have our being." We are in God, and God is within us. We have the right to do as we please; but it is the power of God within us that enables us to see, smell, taste, feel, move, take pictures and interpret them, and enjoy life.

The realization that the perfect spiritual man with his perfect spiritual (eternal) body is delivering power, growth, activity, and life to the physical man clears the mind of dual-mindedness and lets us understand that spiritual insight and good physical eyesight are the inside and outside of the same cup.

To see only the good in people, things, and conditions will help wonderfully in restoring physical eyesight to normal, because the dropping of the good seed thought into the soil of the subconscious mind results in the coming forth in the physical body of that which man desires. The subconscious nature of man, which is the servant of both the conscious and the spiritual phase of mind, can restore perfect functioning and structure to the physical eyes so that they can again become the perfect cameras through which man sees. By declaring the

Truth often; by stopping all enervating practices that have used energy wastefully, particularly excessive sexual indulgence, overeating, smoking, drinking alcoholic liquors; and by doing personal prayer work, man can demonstrate perfect physical sight for himself.

Use the following affirmations:

———

God gave me perfect sight and I will never lose it. Divine intelligence illumines my mind and guides me in every habit of living. Divine love harmonizes all my relationships with humans, animals, and nature, and I see the beauty of God in manifestation everywhere.

———

Criticism and condemnation leave my soul and life. Love and Truth

shine through my mind, eyes, and
every part of my body.

People, things, and conditions
have no power to disturb me. I see
through all false conditions to the
Truth of God and I am at peace.

How to Use Your Memory

MEMORY is the ability of the conscious part of man (often called the intellectual or conscious mind) to bring up at will from the subconsciousness the stored images of thoughts and feelings of the past. The subconscious mind contains all that we have thought, said, and done in the past, and has been called the "seat of memory." When we say we forget something, we mean that we have failed to get into the hidden shelves in the subconsciousness or have failed to find the record we wish to bring up.

How often have we said (when asked a question), "I know the answer and will remember it in a minute"— and shortly (if we hold the conscious mind in abeyance) the answer will "pop up" and we say, "See, I knew it all the time!"

The subconscious mind is the servant of the conscious phase of mind and can be trained to express what we desire to keep as memory records, to radiate perfect control, and to rebuild the physical body. Many persons, because of improper living habits, find it difficult to "think through" any experience. Such conditions, however, can be corrected through the study of Truth to impress the subconsciousness.

The conscious phase of mind can tell the subconscious mind to accept from God (or spiritual man) what God directs, and the conscious phase of mind can also relax and receive direct from God within.

To train the memory, use the following affirmations:

———

I am a perfect spiritual being and I need never forget anything.

———

I recall from my subconscious

mind what I wish to remember at
the time I wish to remember it.

My memory is a gift from God,
ever ready to serve me.

How to Overcome Fears

WHAT we understand we do not fear. We gain spiritual understanding through the study of Truth, and when we have built a consciousness of confidence and trust in God, we become courageous souls, easily meeting all that is opposed to the kingdom of God. We dissolve or rise above everything we formerly feared. Personal thought is the mighty weapon that we wield in passing through, dissolving, or destroying false conditions.

How is this done? It is done by doing what Hosea told Israel to do: "Take with you words, and return unto Jehovah: say unto him, Take away all iniquity, and accept that which is good."

Every one of us was given thinking ability when God created us. What we think tends to come into expression through and around us. Most people think of themselves as physical bodies, having minds at the mercy of all that is seen, heard, or felt. Just the opposite is true: we are spiritual beings with thinking ability and what we think we can demonstrate or bring to pass.

The greatest master of all, Jesus Christ, taught clearly the truth about man's relationship to God, his fellow man and nature. Jesus' mighty words clothed many divine principles and ideas with form. We can do the same if we unfold our hidden spiritual powers as He did.

When feeling fearful of anything or any person, stop and deliberately repeat (silently or aloud) statements like the following:

———

I am not afraid of .... [name condition or person]. What I have been seeing or feeling is only a picture in my mind; I now dissolve it and see myself as God sees me—intelligent, kind, loving, peaceful, courageous, powerful, prosperous, happy, protected, guided, and free.

———

Remember the importance of repeating statements until a *feeling* of confidence wells up from the subconsciousness.

Other statements which have been used often in Unity Training School classes are:

———

"I am not afraid of anything,
  Through life I freely roam.
  The world was made for everyone,
  I make myself at home."

(This can be sung to the tune of "Auld Lang Syne")   ———

I let go of all past human ancestral fears, fears about sickness, sex-

ual fears, poverty fears, religious
fears about death or the hereafter,
fears about war, fears about old age.

———

God in the midst of me is mighty
to heal anything in me, anywhere,
any time, and is doing it now.

How to Find Your Right Work

TO find congenial employment is the desire of millions of people. They usually hope that someone will offer them work that they can do easily, and for which they will receive an unusually large financial compensation. More money, more freedom, more power over one's fellow men are the ideals which many men consider proper.

The effort to attain these ideals in physical life is usually made by working strenuously at a job for a while; watching for a chance to be promoted to another job; using every means at hand to "influence the boss"; cutting expenses to meet a family budget; saving a part of the income; seeking the financial advice of those "in the know"; and so on.

When, through an unexpected change of circumstances, employment suddenly stops, what then? The average man starts seeking again "in the without," in the world of affairs, for a job—watching newspaper ads, asking his fellow men if they know of a job, going to an employment agency to find something "suitable."

If a job does not materialize soon, fear seems to drift into his soul and the thought may come: "Why don't I have congenial work? I want to work; why doesn't someone hire me and pay me well?"

The one who continues to go through such experiences as these has never discovered that the Power which created him and permitted him to incarnate in a physical body on earth is within him, waiting to be recognized, willing to answer his questions, eager to place him in work that will release his soul faculties and bring him adequate financial compensation.

To discover this Power which will surely guide one into congenial work with adequate recompense, it is necessary for man to discover his real Self, to be "born anew" as Jesus put it—to rise in consciousness or think above the problem.

Thought discipline is the secret of success—and discipline over depressed feelings and unhappy conditions in life comes as one studies what God (Divine Mind) is; where God is; how God works; man's relationship to God; what man is, and his relation to his fellow man.

A definite prayer statement (or affirmation) which "connects" with the Source of power within and releases guidance and opportunity, is the thought instrument to use in the emergency of unemployment. Say repeatedly, morning, noon, and night, the following:

———

God, the Power within that brought me into the world, is guid-

ing and directing me, and a quick
contact is made with the work God
has for me to do.

———

Expect the answer—and the opportunity will appear.

How to Have Abundant Supply

ONE of the rich attributes of God is *substance*. Substance underlies and penetrates everything in the physical, mental, and spiritual planes. In fact, substance is everywhere present as part of Universal Mind (often called the God-creative Mind.) Man was created by God as a spiritual being, expressing in a physical body, with unlimited freedom of thought, but man generally has forgotten this and used his mind to please his sense nature. Through the false use of mind (or ignorance of his birthright from God) man has produced conditions of poverty, lack, and unhappiness for himself. Thought creates mental images, molds substance into form, thereby invoking hidden laws to act through substance. Man's thinking therefore produces prosperity or poverty, or a mixture of both from time to time. The dual phase of mind called the human mind often sees both sides of conditions in physical life but usually does not know how to become single-minded or unified in the use of thought.

The person who can receive ideas of plenty from God within and keep his conscious phase of mind sending instructions to his subconscious mind to produce an abundant supply of all good for himself, has reached that stage in unfolding the Truth wherein he will never lack.

The money system of the world is a convenient way of evaluating services, commodities, and goods, and when understood and used righteously it will bring splendid returns in prosperous living. Since the earth is made of substance and all money is coined or printed on the physical things of the earth (metal, wood, and paper) it can truly be said that man has a subconscious contact with God-substance, in the form of money as well as in service to humanity.

The following prayer statements can be used to educate the mind and subconsciously to set prosperity laws into action:

God directs me to my right work which is valuable to mankind and joyfully paid for.

I work for God to promote His good and He rewards me abundantly.

The work I can do and no one else can do, the job I can fill and no one else can fill, is given me by the Spirit, and I do the work perfectly to the glory of God and the good of man.

I picture myself having plenty of God-substance to use as God directs.

———

Divine substance fills my mind, my pocketbook, my bank account to overflowing and I always have plenty to spare and to share.

———

From all directions, in perfect ways, come large sums of God-substance in money form for my personal use and I use it wisely.

———

No human thought, no human being can prevent my becoming increasingly prosperous.

———

I always give more in constructive service than is expected, thereby helping my fellow man enjoy life more.

———

I always remember to tithe my gross financial income to help promote God's work on earth under God's direction.

———

I hold no one in debt to me financially and no one holds me in debt.

———

In all financial dealings (as well as in other ways) I obey the Golden Rule. I see God in action on both sides of all business dealings.

———

I never limit another's prosperity by a restricting thought.

I am willing that everyone else should have a financial income such as I would like for myself.

———

God responds to my prayers concerning spiritual prosperity, investments, pensions, travel.

———

I claim appreciation from God for all good work well done and my soul is at peace.

How to Release God-Power
through Singing

A NYONE who can speak can sing.
Of course, some sound better
than others, but music is a gift of God
to all, and only awaits man's recog-
nition, cultivation, and use.

The statement "Music has charms to
soothe a savage breast" is based on
truth. Music can soothe hurt feelings
and stimulate men and women to great
efforts of different kinds.

Witness the effect of martial music
on soldiers in wartime, and the wonderful effects produced on thousands
of people at operas, concerts, and over
radio and television. In religious meet-
ings, a skilled leader of songs and
hymns can produce almost any kind of
an emotional mass response desired.

The race mind has billions of musi-
cal vibrations of notes and word pictures in it, and up from our personal

subconsciousness at times come (through memory) many of the old familiar songs.

Personal spiritual unfoldment of Truth students through the use of the "word" silently or aloud can be greatly speeded up by the use of songs; by putting constructive words to the music of popular tunes, and some of the old ballads and religious melodies.

A splendid practice is to consider the meaning of the words of prayer songs; then gently or vigorously (according to the effect desired) sing the verse or verses (perhaps repeating several times); then relax and gently hum the tune (thinking of the words). Humming produces a vibration over the nerves and through the glands and bones of the body, often healing conditions quickly. It is important to train the subconscious mind only with constructive words.

Songs Used in Unity Training School Exercise Classes

1. Beautiful Spirit, waken in me,
   Beautiful Spirit, now waken in me.
   Beautiful Spirit, waken in me,
   Beautiful Spirit, now waken in me.
   Beautiful Spirit, waken in me,
   Beautiful Spirit, awaken in me.
   Beautiful Spirit, waken in me,
   Beautiful Spirit, now waken in me.
   Beautiful Spirit, now waken in me.

   Music: "Beautiful Dreamer."

2. Blessed Spirit, fill me
   With Thy love right now.
   Blessed Spirit, fill me
   With Thy love right now.
   Blessed Spirit, fill me
   With Thy love right now.
   Blessed Spirit, fill me
   With Thy love right now,
   With Thy love right now.

Music: Chorus of "Love's Old Sweet
            Song."

3. All hurt feelings now have left me,
   All hurt feelings now have gone;
   All hurt feelings now have left me,
   All hurt feelings now have gone.

   Chorus

   I am filled with God's great love
      now,
   I am filled with God's great love;
   I am filled with God's great love
      now,
   I am filled with God's great love.

Music: "Let the Lower Lights Be
      Burning."

4. From God comes great love,
    His mighty love for me,
    It flows through me now,
    It flows through me now,
    His mighty love for me.
    From God comes great love,
    His mighty love for me,
    It flows through me now,
    It flows through me now,
    His mighty love for me.

Music: "My Wild Irish Rose."

5. God's wisdom is ever within me,
    God's wisdom is ever in me.
    God's wisdom is ever within me,
    God's wisdom is ever in me.

        Chorus

    Wisdom, wisdom,
    God's wisdom is ever in me, in me,
    Wisdom, wisdom,
    God's wisdom is ever in me.

Music: "Bring Back My Bonnie."

—

6. God's love is deep within me,
    Ever satisfying my soul.
    God's love is deep within me,
    Ever satisfying my soul.

Music: "Swing Low, Sweet Chariot."

7. I'm filled with Thy love this fine
   day, Spirit,
   I'm filled with Thy love this fine
   day.

   (Repeat both lines over and over.)

Music: "When You and I Were
Young, Maggie."

---

8. I am calm, I am still,
   I'm fulfilling God's will.

   (Repeat to end of song.)

   Music: "Brahms' Lullaby."

---

9. I am free from confusion,
   I am free from confusion,
   I am free from confusion,
   Every day I am renewed.

   (Repeat if desired.)

Music: "The Old Time Religion."

10. I am free from limitation,
     I am filled with inspiration,
     All the channels for my good are
        open now.
     I am free from limitation,
     I am filled with inspiration,
     All the channels for my good are
        open now.

     Chorus

     Oh, it's great, oh, it's great,
     Oh, it's great to feel so free.
     I am free from limitation,
     I am filled with inspiration,
     All the channels for my good are
        open now.

Music: "Polly-Wolly-Doodle."

11. I am full of joy and sunshine,
     All the livelong day.

    (Repeat to end of song.)

Music: "I've Been Working on the
         Railroad."

---

12. I am happy, joyous, free now all
     the time;
     I am happy, joyous, free now all
     the time;
     I am happy, joyous, free now,
     I am happy, joyous, free now,
     I am happy, joyous, free now all
     the time.

Music: "She'll Be Comin' 'Round the
        Mountain."

13. I am loving and kind,
    I am loving and kind,
    I am loving and kind all the time.
    I am loving and kind,
    I am loving and kind,
    I am loving and kind all the time.

    Chorus

    Loving and kind,
    I am loving and kind all the time.
    I am loving and kind,
    I am loving and kind,
    I am loving and kind all the time.

    Music: "Home on the Range."

---

14. I am now free,
    I am now free,
    I am, I am now free.

    (Repeat to end of song.)

Music: "Drink to Me Only with Thine
              Eyes."

15. I am the radiant life of God,
     I live so joyously,
     I am the radiant life of God,
     I live so joyously,
     I am the radiant life of God,
     I live so joyously,
     I am the radiant life of God,
     I live so joyously.

Chorus

Oh, sing hallelujah, tra, la, la, la,
   la, la, la,
Oh, sing hallelujah, tra, la, la, la,
   la,la, la, la, la.

(Repeat verse.)

Music: "Solomon Levi."

16. I can see perfectly,
     I can see perfectly,
     I can see perfectly all the time.
     I can see perfectly,
     I can see perfectly,
     I can see perfectly all the time.

Chorus

Praise God I can see,
I can see perfectly all the time,
I can see perfectly, I can see per-
     fectly,
I can see perfectly all the time.

Music: "Home on the Range."

---

17. I do to others what I would
     Have others do to me,
     I do to others what I would
     Have others do to me.

(Repeat to end of song.)

Music: "Auld Lang Syne."

18. I feel God's joy, joy, joy, joy
    Down in my heart,
    Down in my heart,
    Down in my heart.
    I feel God's joy, joy, joy, joy,
    Down in my heart,
    Down in my heart today.

Music: "Joy in My Heart."

(From "Pinebrook Choruses: The Young People's Church of the Air." Music copyrighted 1925 by George W. Cooke.)

———

19. I give and receive
    Of the substance of God.

    (Repeat to end of song.)

Music: "Flow Gently, Sweet Afton."

20. I have such a wonderful memory,
    I have such a wonderful mind,
    I have such a wonderful memory,
    I have such a wonderful mind.

Chorus

Praise God, praise God,
I have such a wonderful memory,
Praise God, praise God,
I have such a wonderful mind.

Music: "My Bonnie Lies over the
           Ocean."

---

21. I love life, I love life,
    I love life today,
    I love life, I love life,
    I love life today.

(Repeat to end of song.)

Music: Chorus of "Jingle Bells."

22. I love to live and I live to love,
     Expressing Christ in me.
     I love to live and I live to love,
     Expressing Christ in me.

Music: "Where Is My Little Dog
          Gone?"

---

23. I'm one with God,
     God's one with me,
     I'm one with God,
     God's one with me.

     (Repeat to end of song.)

     Music: "Sweet Genevieve."

24. I'm so relaxed and so happy,
    I'm so relaxed and so gay,
    I'm so relaxed and so happy,
    Everything's going God's way.

Music: Chorus of "Oh, What a Beautiful Morning."

(Music copyrighted 1943 by Williamson Music, Inc., New York, N. Y.)

---

25. I now am courageous, courageous,
       courageous,
    I now am courageous, courageous,
       today.
    I now am courageous, courageous,
       courageous,
    I now am filled with health and
       strength,
    I'm strong and well.

Music: "The Bells of St. Mary's."

(Music copyrighted 1917 by Ascherberg, Hopwood, and Crew, Ltd., London, England.)

26. I radiate God's love,
   I radiate God's love,
   More every day.
   I radiate God's love,
   I radiate God's love,
   I radiate God's love,
   More every day.

   Music: "America."

---

27. Joyous health and healing power
   Vibrate through me every hour.
   Joyous health and healing power
   Vibrate through me every hour.

   (Repeat to end of song.)

Music: "Hark! the Herald Angels Sing."

28. Oh, I'm sure to sleep
    The whole night through,
    I'm sure to sleep all night.
    I'm sure to sleep the whole night
        through,
    I'm sure to sleep all night.

Music: "It Ain't Gonna Rain."

29. Oh, life is great,
    I ain't like I used to be,
    Ain't like I used to be,
    Ain't like I used to be.
    Oh, life is great,
    I'm thrilled as I never was,
    Filled with harmony.

Music: "The Old Gray Mare."

30. There's a glad song in my heart
    today,
    And I cannot be sad;
    Christ in my life now reveals the
    way,
    Oh, say but I'm glad.

    Chorus

    Oh, say but I'm glad, I'm glad,
    Oh, say but I'm glad;
    Joy now has come and my cup's
    overrun,
    That's why I am glad.

Music: "Oh, Say but I'm Glad."

31. Sweep over my soul,
     Sweep over my soul,
     Come, Gracious Spirit,
     Sweep over my soul.

Music: "Sweep over My Soul."

(From "Pinebrook Choruses." Music copy-
     righted 1927 by Harry D. Clarke)

32. The more we get together,
     Together, together,
     The more we get together,
     The happier we'll be.
     For your friends are my friends,
     And my friends are your friends,
     The more we get together,
     The happier we'll be.

Music: "The More We Get Together."

33. The sickness germ is not for me,
     For I am well,
     The sickness germ is not for me,
     For I am well;
     The sickness germ is not for me,
     For I'm as well as I can be,
     Health and power flow through
       me.

Music: Chorus of "Hinky, Dinky,
         Parlez Vous."

---

34. God's Spirit lives in me,
     God's Spirit lives in me,
     Radiating through each cell,
     God's Spirit lives in me.

     Music: "Farmer in the Dell."

Hints about Physical Exercise

MANY persons who come into Truth study become so enthusiastic over the teaching that God is all and in all that they forget the human responsibility of caring for their physical bodies. As years pass, these persons usually show their neglect of their physical bodies in their gradual slowing down of thought and action, and often find themselves seeking relief from pains, aches, impaired functioning, and decaying structures. People who grow old or decrepit do not fully understand how to apply Truth.

Physical bodies are renewed (according to science) every eleven months—the idea being that this includes the nine-month period of gestation required to produce the normal infant body, and two additional months for further development of hair and teeth, and alimentary changes. The undesired changes that take place in the organism are induced more through beliefs in age and sickness and neglect of proper living and thinking habits than in any other way. If one grows old and stiff through failure to exercise the body normally, or if he fails in his own prayers to seek guidance about living habits, the result is the same.

Those who have become wise are particular to exercise the joints and muscles of their bodies every day, sufficiently to induce a normal flow of blood and to breathe in more life force from the air. Thus food intake, nutrition, and elimination are balanced functions with the mind as director.

Exercises Used in Unity Training School Exercise Classes

Statement: I thank God for perfect life flowing freely through every cell of my body.

(Repeat each exercise four to sixteen times.)

1. Take a sitting position; extend arms at side and flex fingers.
2. Extend arms downward, bend at elbows, bringing hands to shoulder and back to position.
3. Raise arms forward, upward, and return.
4. Arms hanging at sides, rotate or turn arms in and out.
5. Hands on knees: bend head forward and backward.
6. Incline head to left and to right.
7. Turn head left and right.
8. Thrust chin forward and back.

Statement: Divine love in me dissolves all irritations and all obstructions in mind and body, and restores perfect motion to every muscle and joint.

9. Circle arms round and round, forward, then backward.

10. Extend arms outward from shoulders, then cross arms over chest, and return.

11. Stand in position at back of chair, with hand on chair. Swing left leg outward sideways and then across in front. Repeat using right leg.

12. With both hands on back of chair, move back from chair. Twist hips left and right, turning on balls of feet.

13. Stand with right side at back of chair, with one hand on chair. Swing left leg forward, upward, and then backward. Repeat using right leg.

Statement: I give thanks to God that my eyes are made perfect.

14. With eyelids closed or open, turn eyeballs up and down.
15. With eyelids closed or open, turn eyeballs left and right.
16. With eyelids closed or open, circle eyeballs left and right.
17. Wink and blink.
18. With the arm extended forward, the gaze concentrated on end of finger, bend arm, bringing finger to nose.
19. Extend both arms forward with forefingers raised. Swing arms gradually outward, left eye looking at left forefinger and right eye looking at right forefinger, until fingers are out of field of vision. Return to position and repeat.

Statement: Through the power of God in me I can see perfectly, near and far, up, down, and round about.

Statement: My digestion, circulation, and elimination are made perfect. I agree with all good food; all good food agrees with me. I select my foods wisely, and I eat not too much and not too little, but just exactly enough for bodily needs.

20. Sitting position, with arms over head: bend downward and forward, touching floor with hands.

21. Start with hands on hips, and bend sideways, left and right, touching floor with hands.

22. Place hands on knees: circle trunk left and right, twisting the backbone.

23. Place hands on hips; stand up; sit down.

24. Breathe in through both nostrils, vibrate diaphragm, expel air.

25. (For ears) Breathe in, hold mouth and nose tightly shut, vi-

brate diaphragm, pumping air
against eardrums.

26. (Spinal exercises) Stretch arms
    over head with hands clasped:
    twist easily left and then right.

27. Clasp hands back of head: turn
    left and right, twisting spine.

Jumping Exercises

(To be performed with discretion.)

28. Jump lightly with both feet, turn-
    ing around left and right.

29. Jump to stride stand, raising arms
    upward at the side and down-
    ward.

Statement: As the years roll on I exercise wisely. I give thanks to God
that I feel renewed and refreshed in
mind and body.

Daily Prayer Map

How to use: Start the day after awaking, and end the day before sleeping, by meditating on each prayer statement you are using to gain the meaning; then whisper it rapidly several times to impress the subconscious nature. Relax the mind a moment to let God have His way; then take up the next statement.

Creation: God, the one and only unchangeable Presence and Power created man from Himself as an individualized, spiritual thinking being. Man has named God Divine Mind, Eternal Life, Love, Truth, Substance, Principle, Law, Lord, Spirit, universal Creator, and Sustainer of all the universe. As man thinks rightly he can use God's ideas, principles and laws to make for himself an enjoyable life.

116

Guidance: As I yield my intellect to the Spirit, divine intelligence illumines my mind, guides me in all studies, and shows me what to think, say and do every day.

Love: Divine love harmonizes me with the good in people, things, and conditions every day and brings to me my own. I love all people, all people love me, without attachment.

Work: Both work and supply come from God. The position of service that I can fill and no one else can fill is given me by the Spirit. I do the work to the glory of God and the good of my fellow man.

Supply: Voluntary, faithful tithing operates the divine law of increasing prosperity for me. Divine substance fills my mind, my pocketbook, my bank account to overflowing and I always have plenty to spare and to share.

Protection: I declare my personal freedom from all unwanted influences, from all racial mind deteriorations, from all possibilities of accidents. I am sensitive, receptive, obedient to Divine Mind ideas only. God is my ever-present protection, within me and surrounding me night and day.

Home: I radiate divine peace, harmony, and Golden Rule action in the mental and physical atmosphere of my home.

Divine Design: "Thou in me doth reveal to me Thy divine design for my life. Thou doth open the way quickly for its manifestation."

Spiritual Education: The study of the teachings of Jesus the Christ, the greatest Master of all; certain Bible passages; and the study of Unity books, courses, and other metaphysical literature, all stimulate me into seeking deeper into the kingdom of God within me first, so that all other good things follow in divine order. I realize the necessity of doing my own personal daily prayer work in order to improve my own subconscious mind, which constantly externalizes what I have put into it.

Peace: The killing of men to please other men, and the killing of animals for human food and clothing are no longer part of my consciousness. The freedom I desire for myself is the freedom I grant to all free-moving, God-created creatures on earth. God-peace, released by my personal thought within myself, assures peace of mind and action for me, and adds to peace in the world.

Appearance: I visualize myself clothed in garments of worth and approval, radiating eternal youth, eternal joy, eternal beauty, eternal health, eternal motion, eternal prosperity, every day.

Memory: My memory is a gift of God to me and I can never lose it. I can remember what I need to remember at the time I wish to remember it.

Golden Rule: I do to others first what I would have others do to me. I do not do for others what they are unwilling to do for themselves. I refuse to accept (consciously or subconsciously) any person's opinion of me not based on the Truth. I no longer hold anyone in bondage with my personal thoughts or feelings or actions. I express and ask for forgiveness whenever necessary. I love my God with all my mind and heart, and I love my neighbor as I love my higher self.

Living Habits: Correct habits of thinking, breathing, eating, drinking, exercising, sleeping, and sun, air, and water bathing are revealed to me by my indwelling Spirit. I obey the Spirit and manifest a vigorous, healthful, peaceful, harmonious life.

Vacation: The Spirit in me reveals to me when, why, how, and where I can go, to relax soul and body, and improve my consciousness at vacation time.

Overcoming Fear: I cast out (consciously and subconsciously) all past fears about sickness, wars, politics, poverty, sex, and religion. I am not afraid of anything past, present, or future. God in me is greater than any human experience and can deliver me from everything that should not be.

Thankful Attitude: Counting my present blessings and praising God in myself and in my neighbor, I experience more of the goodness of God every day.

Life Beyond: I realize I am a perfect spiritual being and can never die. I always have and always will live eternally somewhere. I realize that I take my spiritual body and consciousness with me to the next plane of existence. I keep improving my consciousness (states of thought and feelings) every day here and now through Truth study, as revealed by the teachings of Jesus Christ. The Truth can guide me ever onward gloriously through God's many worlds of life.

Healing Prayer: God, my Indwelling Spirit, heals me perfectly while I sleep and I awaken refreshed in the morning.

Questions and Answers

Repetition of Affirmations

Question

Why do some Truth teachers advocate the repeating of affirmations, while others scoff at such a practice?

Answer

As Jesus said, "By their fruits ye shall know them."

It is possible to produce wonderful results or demonstrations by just "speaking the word" once, provided that the one doing the speaking has an illumined consciousness and great faith. Few persons have reached such a stage of consciousness, however. Most persons have subconscious blocks, hidden feelings and beliefs of which they are often unaware. These persons need training like little children in order to gain control over the hidden subconscious part of themselves, and repetition starts a new vibration through the subconscious mind which will prove itself. One has only to try out the repeated-affirmation method in order to prove to himself whether or not it works for him.

"He that ruleth his spirit [his sub-conscious] [is greater] than he that taketh a city."

Appreciation

Question

I am not appreciated by my family or friends, even though I am always doing nice things for them. How can I gain their appreciation?

Answer

To expect others to do as you wish them to do may bring antagonism into your life even though your outward acts seem beneficial.

Claim appreciation for your good work from God, not from humans. In all human relationships ask God to direct you, and you will not be doing things for others which many times they might prefer to do for themselves. We do not have the right to interfere with another's physical actions unless our own rights are being interfered with.

Say often:

Divine intelligence and divine

love govern me in all human relationships; my soul is satisfied in God's way and I am rewarded by the Spirit. I appreciate God and spiritual man, and I am appreciated.

Right or Wrong Thinking and Acting

Question

How can I know the difference between right and wrong thinking and acting?

Answer

Everything begins with thought. Each person has freedom to think as he pleases. Thinking controls all action, and all physical activity. Responsibility for thinking is something that each individual must assume, sooner or later.

If what you are thinking comes into form or action in a way to benefit everybody, it must be right or correct (based on divine principle).

If what you think would injure, interfere, or hurt anyone else when it comes into form or action, it must be erroneous or incorrect.

Therefore, study Truth and learn to

think constructively (for the good of all, yourself included).

The only thing that is always right is the right, perfect action of Divine Mind, which is always taking place through spiritual man. Therefore, link up your human phase of mind with the divine by saying often:

I let the mind of God direct my thinking, and I find myself doing the right thing at the right time in the right way, governed by God. I am at peace always.

Arguing

Question

I have attended Truth classes for several years, and I often get into arguments about Bible meanings and the teachings of Jesus. I feel irritated and exhausted afterward. How can I get over this?

Answer

Everyone is entitled to his own opinions concerning such things. To try to convince someone against his will is a waste of time. All religious philosophies have a place and serve a purpose. The Truth of God and spiritual man is unchangeable and eternal, regardless of human opinions. Truth is discovered by turning thought inward to God and asking for illumination. Illumination (or wisdom) flows back through man, revealing the Truth which never needs argument to be proved. Say often:

I grant freedom to all persons regardless of their religious concepts, and claim my own freedom to seek and practice the Truth, which reveals itself to me more every day. I bless all teachings of the past that have helped mankind, and I am at peace.

Being Entertained

Question

I want to make spiritual progress but I find myself looking at television programs for hours, spending much time in motion picture shows, and yearning often to be with people just to "discuss things." How can I get over this?

Answer

The divine design of everyone's earth life contains health, wealth, love, and opportunities to express one's spiritual self. All of these wonderful ideas or gifts of God are in the soul, awaiting expression or manifestation. The spoken word will release them.

The senses of man, through which he is related to the outside world, often become the masters instead of the servants. Jesus' instructions were that men should enter the "inner chamber," close the door, and pray in secret to the Father, who rewards openly.

We are therefore to stop looking at, hearing, and talking about outside things, and instead to commune with the Spirit, the Father within, asking for and waiting to receive a response. "Where thy treasure is, there will thy heart be also." Seeking the God-power within first and letting It direct one's life will soon overcome the desire to "be entertained" so that worth-while character and activities will manifest. This does not mean that all worldly pleasures are to be given up, but that the whole man—Spirit, soul, and body—should reflect divine guidance.

Say often:

I desire only that which is conducive to my spiritual progress.

The Fear of Death

Question

Although I have lived for many years and have read all kinds of explanations about the "hereafter," I still quake with fear whenever I think of what may happen to me in years to come. Can this fear be eliminated?

Answer

No one knows how many years of mortal life he will go through, although he usually hopes that they will be many. Some persons believe that they can expect to live for threescore years and ten, because the Bible says that is man's span of life. Others work diligently in controlling body habits, hoping to extend their years beyond one hundred. Some believe it is possible to refine flesh cells until the cells become spiritual, undying substance, and thereby live as long as they desire. Some metaphysical students believe

that it is possible for the mortal to
"put on immortality" through human
desires; others believe that man, created by God as an eternal, immortal
being with an eternal, immortal, spiritual body, can live in any place of
life he desires, being superior to earth,
air, fire, and water.

Many persons have written books
expressing their personal opinions
about life hereafter. Many religions
have come into being on earth, pur-
porting to teach what should or should
not be done to have a life of harmony
and peace here or hereafter.

Jesus Christ instructed His hearers
about life in the invisible realm, as
well as the necessity of each person's
learning more of Truth while living
in a body of flesh here in this world.

"Flesh and blood cannot inherit the
kingdom of God." This is a statement
that is often ignored and seldom explained by metaphysical teachers.

Each person who is sincerely interested in having revealed to him the truth about life and death can learn from the Spirit within himself what is true if he will follow Hosea's instructions to Israel, "Take with you words, and return unto Jehovah."

As a favorite Truth writer, Zelia M. Walters, has put it: "Of one thing we feel sure: God is a God of love, and there are no fires of hell or eternal punishment for man to experience. So there is nothing to fear in this respect. . . . In faith let us leave this search for a description of what will be. Jesus bade us be concerned with the call of today. The morrow is in God's loving care."

A prayer like the following will bring satisfaction and confidence to the soul:

The same mind that is in Christ Jesus is in me. All I need to know is clearly revealed to my conscious-

ness and I rejoice in my continuous, eternal ongoing through any world in which I am living or shall live. I let God's will be done in me; I am fearless and free and always at peace within myself.

The Debt Habit

Question

I have been in debt financially all my life. How can I get out of debt?

Answer

Your subconscious nature keeps reproducing the same patterns of life and activity, mentally and physically, over and over, unless you change the patterns. God is the one and only unchangeable power and substance, and He is ever ready to respond to man's righteous use of thought. Make it a habit to treat yourself several times daily, using the following words, whispering them over and over hundreds of times:

I wipe out all subconscious images of debts, past and present. I see myself a prosperous person with all my needs abundantly supplied. I live within my present income and tithe my earnings to some form of God's work. From all directions God's supply comes to me in God's perfect ways and I am at peace.

Remember, mental work (the use of your mind) is required. God loves a diligent thinker.

The Gossip Habit

Question

Often I find myself listening to, agreeing or disagreeing with, people who like to gossip about their friends. How can I train myself to stop gossiping?

Answer

All of us were given freedom of thought when God created us, but few of us have realized our personal responsibility involved in using thought. All that we think, say, and do registers in our subconscious nature and comes forth again by the law of attraction, to bless or to injure us or others.

A Truth student who realizes his personal responsibility for thinking discovers that what he thinks frees or binds him. So he studies Truth to learn better ways of thinking, and thereby frees himself from many unhappy experiences.

If caught in a gossipy "talkfest," simply keep thinking thoughts similar to the following:

What is being said here is of no consequence to me. The perfect action of God is taking place here through all concerned and only Divine Mind ideas are being contacted and expressed. Kindness, love, generosity, and understanding manifest through and for all, myself included.

The result will be that your own soul will not be contaminated, the so-called "gossips" will soon stop gossiping, no one's reputation will suffer, and peace for all will prevail.

The Fast-Driving Habit

Question

I find I am driving my car faster and faster on highways. I realize this may be dangerous. How can I change this habit?

Answer

Letter a sign reading, "The safety of God is omnipresent and I am safe," and place it on your car's sun visor where it can be seen. Every time you get in the car, whisper the words several times. Within a few days you should have transferred the safety word-image into your subconscious mind, which operates your body, and the habit of safe driving will become "second nature."

The Swearing Habit

Question

How can I overcome the habit of swearing?

Answer

Swearing is the result of deep-seated subconscious frustrations, fears, or resentments concerning people, things, or conditions in life.

God made man to express, and gave him freedom of thought and action. That very freedom of thought and action brings experiences into man's life, and sooner or later, by means of these experiences (good or bad), man finds out that he is accountable for every word, feeling, or vibration that passes through or from him. "By thy words thou shalt be justified, and by thy words shalt thou be condemned."

Therefore, the study of Truth (which is learned by thinking, speaking, and acting based on spiritual ideas) becomes the most important thing in the life of anyone who desires to progress spiritually.

Since swearing is usually involved with deep-seated error feelings, one should use the following statement for deliverance, whispering the words repeatedly for several minutes and thereby generating a feeling of release:

I let go every condemning thought or feeling or action. I let the serenity, intelligence, and love of God direct my mind, cleansing it of all blasphemy, and I am at peace with people, things, and conditions at all times.

The Overeating Habit

Question

How can I conquer the habit of overeating?

Answer

The hidden desire in the subconscious mind of certain persons to get more, have more, hold on to more, often works out through the appetite. God intends that the divine law of giving and receiving shall operate so that the inflow and outflow of life and substance are balanced in mind and body and affairs. However, the belief that life is in food and one must eat much to live; the belief that unless one takes much of the manifested substance he will not get his share, tend (in the subconscious mind) to produce a greedy condition in living. This condition often governs the appetite, resulting in excessive eating.

All physical excesses can be corrected in the mind, and thereby external conditions of bondage can be changed. Say often:

Divine intelligence, which knows all, guides me in all my thinking and living habits. I let go all desires for unnecessary food and I eat only what my body needs.

Sincere Truth students who will faithfully repeat the affirmation several times before meals will soon see results.

The Habit of Criticizing

Question

How can I stop being critical?

Answer

It takes no particular degree of intelligence to complain and find fault. When we do so, we often find ourselves the objects of criticism.

We get back through our own subconscious nature that which we send out toward others. If we make critical remarks, they react back to or through us faithfully.

We can change our consciousness whenever we really wish to.

Stop the critical expression coming through your mind by an instant change of thought. If you find yourself saying, "I don't see why he does not do so and so," "I dislike his attitude and actions," "He should not have health or plenty," or any other critical remark, just use your will deliberately to cut the sentence off. Say over and over something that is constructive or helpful. Controlling your mind by letting God guide your thinking into channels of intelligence and love will heal the false habit quickly. Love attracts love.

This prayer will help you:

Granting freedom to all and seeing and praising the good in all, I have an enjoyable life.

The Smoking Habit

Question

How can I give up the smoking habit?

Answer

By changing your consciousness (states of thought and feeling). Smokers are usually in bondage to the subconscious race mind. Clever advertising during the past fifty years has made millions of people believe the claims that tobacco companies make about smoking. One who sincerely desires to give up the smoking habit should convince his own subconscious mind of the truth about spiritual mastership, peace, and health by whispering to himself hundreds of times at daily prayer periods:

I am sensitive, receptive, obedient only to God-Mind ideas which produce health, peace, and comfort through my mind and body. I cast

out all racial mind dominion. I am freed from all desire to smoke and I enjoy my spiritual mastership here and now.

The Alcoholic Habit

Question

How can I break the alcoholic habit?

Answer

Fermenting thoughts and feelings in the mind produce fermenting conditions in the body. Like attracts like. The extensive use of fermented grains and fruits produces a poisoning of the front brain (the organ of the conscious mind) and then the subconscious mind takes over and a "spree" or "jag" of intoxication is the result. The tremendous desire thousands of people have to escape from unwanted situations in physical life, or to become stimulated for a while in order to boast or act courageously (without reasoning), causes them to drink liquor until conscious control of the mind and body is set aside and the subconscious mind, filled with the unsatisfied desires of the past, can act "with the brakes off."

The various clubs and societies that have been founded to help alcoholics tend to help the sufferer to "help himself through helping others" but the real help comes from the Christ *in man* being released into fuller control of mind and body individually.

A powerful affirmation like the following has helped thousands to rise above all alcoholic temptations:

Using the same power that Jesus Christ used and uses, I cast out of my subconscious mind every detrimental influence, and I express my spiritual nature fully through my mind and body. I am always in perfect control of my appetite, and I am at peace.

Publisher's Announcement

Special Methods for Attaining Spiritual Mastery is published by the Unity School of Christianity, an independent educational institution devoted to teaching the principles of Christianity and the application of these principles to everyday life and affair. In addition to *Special Methods for Attaining Spiritual Mastery* Unity School publishes the following other books:

ATOM-SMASHING POWER OF MIND, *by Charles Fillmore*

BE! *by James Dillet Freeman*

BE OF GOOD COURAGE, *by Frank B. Whitney*

BEGINNING AGAIN, *by Frank B. Whitney*

BEST-LOVED UNITY POEMS, *an anthology*

BOTH RICHES AND HONOR, *by Annie Rix Militz*

CHRIST ENTHRONED IN MAN, *by Cora Fillmore*

CHRISTIAN HEALING, *by Charles Fillmore*

DIVINE REMEDIES, *a compilation*

DOCTOR HOUSTON SPEAKING, *by Zelia M. Walters*

EFFECTUAL PRAYER, *by Frances W. Foulks*

FAVORITE UNITY RADIO TALKS, *a collection*

GOD A PRESENT HELP, *by H. Emilie Cady*

GOD IS THE ANSWER, *by Dana Gatlin*

GREAT PHYSICIAN, THE, *by Ernest C. Wilson*

HAVE WE LIVED BEFORE? *by Ernest C. Wilson*

HOW I USED TRUTH, *by H. Emilie Cady*

HOW TO LET GOD HELP YOU, *by Myrtle Fillmore*

JESUS CHRIST HEALS, *by Charles Fillmore*

KEEP A TRUE LENT, *by Charles Fillmore*

KNOW THYSELF, *by Richard Lynch*

LESSONS IN TRUTH, *by H. Emilie Cady*

LET THERE BE LIGHT, *by Elizabeth Sand Turner* ($2)

LOVINGLY IN THE HANDS OF THE FATHER, *by Evelyn Whitell*

MIGHTIER THAN CIRCUMSTANCE, *by Frank B. Whitney*

MORE WONDERFUL YOU, A, *a collection*

MYRTLE FILLMORE'S HEALING LETTERS, *a collection*

MYSTERIES OF GENESIS, *by Charles Fillmore* ($2)

MYSTERIES OF JOHN, *by Charles Fillmore*

NEW WAYS TO SOLVE OLD PROBLEMS, *by Lowell Fillmore*

PEACE BEGINS AT HOME, *by Clara Beranger*

PRACTICAL CHRISTIANITY FOR YOU, *by James E. Sweaney*

PRAYER CHANGES THINGS, *by Dana Gatlin*

PRAYER IN THE MARKET PLACE, *a collection*

PROSPERITY, *by Charles Fillmore*

PROSPERITY'S TEN COMMANDMENTS, *by Georgiana Tree West*

PROVE ME NOW, *by Gardner Hunting*

SELECTED STUDIES, *by Imelda Octavia Shanklin*

STORY OF UNITY, THE, *by James Dillet Freeman*

SUNLIT WAY, THE, *by Ernest C. Wilson*

TALKS ON TRUTH, *by Charles Fillmore*

TEACH US TO PRAY, *by Charles and Cora Fillmore*

These books cover so many subjects of general and vital interest that among them you are sure to find one that meets a need of your own or that of a friend. Beautifully bound, gilt stamped, these lovely books are priced at $1 each unless otherwise indicated.

UNITY SCHOOL OF CHRISTIANITY
Lee's Summit, Mo.

PRINTED U.S.A.   65F-7M-8-68